For all the
'brilliant' pupils at

MJS

please read and
then put the habits
into practice!

ENJOY!

GW00646391

A Brilliant Life

First published in 2008 by Balloon View Ltd
Regents Place, 338 Euston Road, London NW1 3BT

This edition published in 2008

Designed and set by Artica Design Services, Eastbourne (01323) 419844

Illustrations by Laura E Martin

Printed for Balloon View by Replika Press Pvt Ltd, Sonipate, India.

Balloon View Ltd
Regents Place
338 Euston Road
London NW1 3BT
www.balloonview.com

A Brilliant Life

Andrew Cope

Andy Cope (it's only his mum who calls him 'Andrew') lives with his wife and two children (Sophie and Ollie) in a village near Derby. He was born the same year that England won the world cup.

Like many authors, he has a proper job that keeps him busy during the day and he writes furiously in his spare time. Andy is a qualified teacher who used to work as a lecturer in Colleges and Universities but he now works for himself training teenagers, teachers, managers and business people. He runs a really fab course called 'The Art of Being Brilliant', which is about positive psychology and generally being the best person you can be. His work takes him all over the world.

Andy has written the highly successful 'Spy Dog' series for Puffin. His first book won the Red House Children's Book Award and he is currently working on book four of a five book series. Andy has also written 'Being Brilliant' aimed at mums, dads and business people.

Andy is a sporting nut and he is especially keen on football. Most of his Saturdays are ruined because he supports Derby County! Andy has a pet dog, Lara, who is the star of his 'Spy Dog' books. He has just acquired two ginger and black piglets for which the word 'cute' is an understatement (and, before you ask, they are pets and are not destined to become hog roasts).

Andy doesn't get much spare time. He tries to follow his children to tennis, trampolining, karate, swimming, netball, rugby and footy, but sometimes goes to the wrong club on the wrong day!

One of Andy's ambitions is to be able to surf, brilliantly.

A BRILLIANT LIFE

ANDREW COPE

There was once a young person
who got by in life.

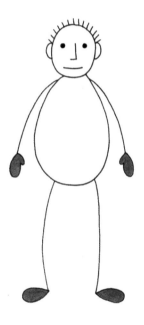

Everything was just kinda OK.

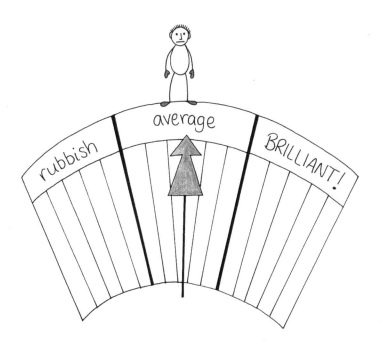

You know, average.

He did alright at school. But he was a teenager and everyone knows that teenagers moan. Life's so unfair. I mean, they've got homework, coursework, exams and school. And everyone struggles to get out of bed, don't they?

Like most teenagers, his negativity had become a habit.

He thought about his negative habits and began to change them.

He learned some stuff – and became brilliant.

This is what he learned.
He called it the 'Big 5.'

It was life-changing.

And he didn't just learn the Big 5...

...he did them. Wow!

First he chose his attitude.

He actually chose to be positive.

Which was very difficult when those around him weren't. Especially in maths.

Everybody else continued to moan that life wasn't fair. But he decided school was an opportunity to get on in life. He would tackle it with a 'can do' attitude.

Next, he learned that when he was positive, nice things happened to him.

The world was great. Lessons were easier. Maths could be fun. Imagine!

And when he was positive he smiled more.
It was kinda weird, but he made others
feel brilliant too.

And when he felt rubbish, so did those around him. Spooky or what?

He'd stumbled upon the second of the 'Big 5'. He realised he was having a huge impact on those around him – much bigger than he'd ever imagined. And he could choose which impact he had. 'Positive' or 'negative'?

Mmmm, tricky one, eh?

And he realised it was the most powerful choice in the world.

(He did wonder why nobody else seemed to be making the right choice, but he didn't let others' negative attitudes stop him feeling brilliant).

Thirdly, he set himself some huge goals.

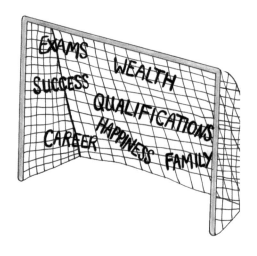

Really big ones that were scary at first.

So he broke them down into little steps and started making them happen.

Strangely enough, a lot of his goals were dependent on how much effort he put into his school work.

And he never gave up on his goals – even when things got tough. Which was often.

He learned something really interesting.
He discovered that even when he did his level
best to be brilliant, things still went wrong.
And sometimes maths was really hard.

Like seriously rock hard.

And he could still end up feeling rubbish.
It was true what teenagers said...

...life wasn't always fair!

But he didn't have many bad days because he'd learned the fourth point of the 'Big 5'.

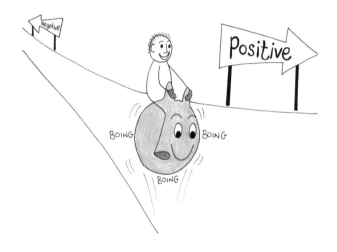

He had 'bouncebackability.'

He'd worked out that an average lifespan would give him 4000 weeks. Sure, this was quite a big number, but it made him realise how valuable time was.

He decided life was too short to waste being anything less than brilliant.

When he caught himself being negative he thought about his 4000 weeks and quickly bungeed back to being positive.

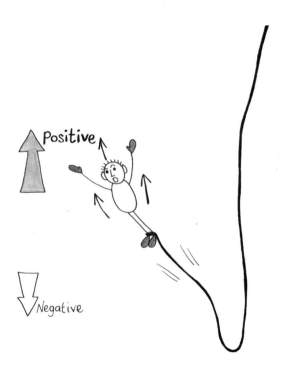

He practised until this became his normal way of thinking.

He now had 4 of the 'Big 5'. He had chosen to be positive, he understood the impact he had, he set big goals and he had bouncebackability.

But the last one was very important. Finally he realised that he had to take responsibility for his life. For teenagers, this was the hardest thing to do!

He noticed others blaming their rubbish life on their teachers and relationships and the fact they didn't have the latest designer clothes.

In fact, the more he listened, the more he heard teenagers blaming everyone but themselves. 'My teachers are rubbish.' 'I've got too much homework.' 'My mum nags me.' 'My dad makes me come home early, it's so unfair.' 'Science is so boring.'

He noticed it was always someone else's fault.

He smiled. He knew his happiness wasn't really about designer clothes.

It was about the choices he made and the
positive attitude he carried with him.

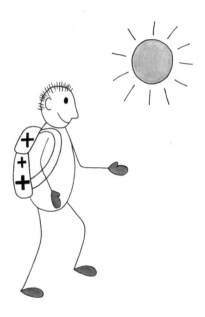

He'd taken personal responsibility for changing
himself. He didn't blame others any more. He
realised it was about taking charge of his life.
He wanted results, not excuses.

So he made a massive breakthrough.
He stopped thinking about the 'Big 5'
and started doing them instead.

At first it was difficult coz the energy vampires
were everywhere.

They were really good at being negative.
In fact they were better than good –
they were experts!

The energy vampires were brilliant at sucking the positive out of every person.
They had a point.

The weather is always rubbish (isn't it?). And the traffic. And then there's school and homework. And everything else. Nightmare!

He practised being positive, even with the energy vampires (he was a brave young man!)

He noticed that the sun shone loads. And the cars sometimes moved at 100mph. And homework was easier if you did your best. And other things were great too.

He tried ever so hard. He was even happy when it rained. Why be upset about the weather?

And the more he tried the easier it became.

And his life changed for the better. He actually wanted to get out of bed.

After all, he had goals to achieve.

Very quickly he became brilliant. Other people
noticed his cheery smile and positive outlook
on life. Teachers noticed. His parents noticed.
His gran was very proud.
Even his friends noticed.

But he noticed most.

And those around him felt brilliant too.

He got some great grades and
a worthwhile career.

And lived to a ripe old age
(well beyond 4000 weeks).

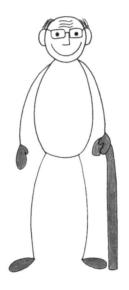

He smiled a lot. His wrinkles were happy.

And he inspired lots of people,
especially his children.

Who turned out brilliant too.

The End

Now for some serious thinking...

1. What is this book about?

2. Who is this book really about?

3. What have you learned?

4. How can you apply it to your life?

5. What would be the result if you did?

6. What's stopping you?

7. Do you want to set your sights on a 'rubbish', 'average' or 'brilliant' life?

8. What do you need to change about yourself to be brilliant?

9. Who are you at your best?

10. Think of someone you really admire. List three qualities that this person has.

11. Think back to the last time you felt brilliant. List six words that describe how you felt.

12. Imagine the perfect you. What kind of person are you? What is your motto in life?

13. If someone was making a speech about you, what would you like them to say?

Challenges

Evidence suggests that most successful people are those who 'dream big' and then take positive action to achieve their goals. Some people get lucky, and achieve success by accident, but most achieve by a combination of positive attitude and action.

1. What do you want to achieve in the next 5 years? Write down your HUGG (Huge Unbelievably Great Goal). List the things you have to do to achieve your goal. What's the first thing you have to do? Do it.

2. Schedule the next things on your list and do them. Keep a list of the actions you have to take and tick them off as you achieve them. Each one will inch you closer to your goal. Review your actions every week so you don't lose sight of your goal.

3. Don't be shy about your goal. Share it with others. Some people (for example, teachers, parents, friends) will be able to help you achieve it.

4. Close your eyes and imagine yourself in five years' time, having achieved your goal. How do you look? What do people say about you? How does your life feel?

5. Take responsibility for changing those aspects of your attitude and personality that you need to change. Remember, if you've become accustomed to being negative, this is just a bad habit. You can break it.

6. Be yourself brilliantly for fourteen days on the trot. After that, it becomes a habit.

This book is based on a workshop called 'The Art of Being Brilliant' that has achieved fantastic results across the world. It has been successful in businesses and schools and is the perfect pick-me-up for anyone between the ages of 12 and 112.

Maybe you would like to know more about the thinking behind the story? Even better, you may want to attend 'The Art of Being Brilliant' or book a session for your school? And it's not just for teenagers – parents and teachers need it just as much.

Alternatively, you may want to share your own brilliant story or tell me what you think of the book. Whatever your reason, please visit www.artofbrilliance.co.uk to find out more. Or, even better, email me direct at: andy@artofbrilliance.co.uk

I look forward to hearing from you.

The Art of Being Brilliant Workshops

Imagine raising your game, enabling the best version of you to shine, consistently. What would your life look, sound and feel like?

Together with my team, I run a workshop called 'The Art of Being Brilliant' which aims to transform the way you think about yourself and your life, inspiring you to make the most of what you've been given and achieve massive personal change. The workshop explores the themes from 'A Brilliant Life', focusing on learning new habits of thinking and behaviour that will sustain your personal 'brilliance'.

'The Art of Being Brilliant' is applicable to everyone, from teenagers to parents, teachers to managers, schools to sports teams, and is designed to be dead simple, totally inspirational and is (dare I say it) rollicking good fun. To book a workshop or to find out more, just check out my website or email me direct – oh and don't worry, I don't bite! *Andy Cope*

'The Art of Being Brilliant' is just one of a series of inspirational courses run by Andy and his team available for schools, businesses and communities. They also offer one-to-one coaching for anyone interested in maximising their potential.

'Outstanding, awesome, brilliant'
Bernard Benjamin

'Brilliant. Have lots to take back and make a difference. I want to make an impact and have a lot of people change to be brilliant as well'
M Honey

'Absolutely awesome experience. Refresher of what is needed to be brilliant. You already know this, now you have to live it'
Nicolene de la Raj

'It was absolutely brilliant! Very inspiring' H Adams
'What can I say apart from WOW!!! BRILLIANT!!!'
Hennie Prinsloo

'Most inspirational and practical course ever' Yolanda
'I am inspired and I WILL make a difference' Joiene Martin
'Excellent, fantastic and brilliant'
Anon

www.artofbrilliance.co.uk andy@artofbrilliance.co.uk

Being Brilliant!
Andrew Cope

If you've selected this book in the hope of finding a conventional step-by-step guide to improving your management skills, I'm afraid you've picked up the wrong book altogether. I fear this book may upset you. It's a story about the stresses of modern life and all the things that can go wrong with work, family, relationships and customers. It's about working too hard and surviving each day in the hope that tomorrow may be better. It's terribly sad, especially when you realise that this book is written about you!

Being Brilliant is for anyone who has a passion to make the most of what they've been given. The underlying message is blindingly simple: Why settle for anything less than being yourself, brilliantly?

"For all our readers who are launching businesses or working in start-up organisations the value of this little book will be self-evident. For everyone else this is a book about going beyond the average and upscaling your aspirations. It is a two hour wake up call that leaves you invigorated and enthusiastic. I feel that I may have been brainwashed because I'm rarely this evangelical about anything (especially not theories of management!) but I really enjoyed entering Cope's world and (you guessed it) I'm feeling brilliant!"

Sarah Barkley –
Transition Tradition.com

Order from www.balloonview.com/personaldevelopment